"Magnificently t   ͵... a delightful empathy with a.. living creatures, makes this an enchanting story about Bryony's recent house guests."

Des Lynam OBE

"In a world that delivers little else but negative news, Bryony Hill's Robins in My Kitchen has been a joy to read. There were days when I believed the robins were nesting in my kitchen so vivid are the descriptions. The company of these birds has uplifted every day. This book, with gorgeous illustrations, is a delight."

Carol Drinkwater, actress, writer and film maker

"Thank you so much. I have so loved the updates on your robins."

Marc Sinden, film maker

"I have loved it Thank you for sharing."

Liz Fielding, author

"I've so enjoyed watching their beautifully captured journey and who knows, that one fledgling could be the one who likes the easy living at home too much to leave…"

Sandra Howard, author

"I particularly love robins, so enjoying this series. It's better than Spring Watch!"

Maggie Alderson, journalist

"As an amateur/garden 'ornithologist' I have adored your bulletins."

James Mossop, sports journalist

"Such a wonderful story Bryony."

Babs and Robert Powell

With best wishes,
Bryony Hill

Robins in My Kitchen

Bryony Hill

The Book Guild Ltd

First published in Great Britain in 2024 by
The Book Guild Ltd
Unit E2 Airfield Business Park,
Harrison Road, Market Harborough,
Leicestershire. LE16 7UL
Tel: 0116 2792299
www.bookguild.co.uk
Email: info@bookguild.co.uk
X: @bookguild

Copyright © 2024 Bryony Hill

The right of Bryony Hill to be identified as the author of this
work has been asserted by them in accordance with the
Copyright, Design and Patents Act 1988.

All rights reserved. No part of this publication may be
reproduced, transmitted, or stored in a retrieval system, in any form or by any means,
without permission in writing from the publisher, nor be otherwise circulated in
any form of binding or cover other than that in which it is published and without
a similar condition being imposed on the subsequent purchaser.

Typeset in 11pt Minion Pro

Printed on FSC accredited paper
Printed and bound in Great Britain by 4edge Limited

ISBN 978 1835740 965

British Library Cataloguing in Publication Data.
A catalogue record for this book is available from the British Library.

If it wasn't for a little robin adopting me as a surrogate grandmother this story would never have been possible. From her first visit to my bedroom before exploring the rest of the house Mrs R, along with Mr R's boundless support, showed their extraordinary confidence and trust in choosing my home in which to raise a family.

"Nothing in the world is quite as adorable as a robin when he shows off and they are nearly always showing off."

Frances Hodgson Burnett,
(1849-1924, *The Secret Garden*)

Introduction

For as long as I can remember I have had a fascination for nature inherited from my parents. During World War Two, my father, who had enlisted in the Royal Naval Volunteer Reserve, remained stationed in Normandy having taken part in the D-Day Landings at Sword Beach and where, billeted in a tent in an apple orchard, he befriended a jackdaw. This is an extract from a letter to his father in Sussex three weeks before Christmas, December 1944:

Jack fed from my hand after brekker [sic]. Jack loves water and I keep a pie dish filled for him. I brought it to his bird table this morning with some new water in it and before it was out of my hand, he had jumped in with great head duckings, flapping and dancing about. I would very much like to bring him home but doubt whether I shall have the chance.

Memories from my childhood are scattered with tales of fledglings rescued, having fallen from the nest or brought into the house as gifts by our cat Timmy Tucker. Kept next to the Aga for warmth in a newspaper-lined cardboard box secured with a cake rack, feeding was unknown territory. Ma navigated the problem by concocting a mixture of scrambled egg and finely chopped worms using her eyebrow tweezers to feed the vulnerable orphans.

Prior to the house opposite undergoing structural work, the rampant Virginia creeper had to be removed from the exterior walls. The doorbell rang and one of the builders stood there, his hands cupping a tiny bird. He explained that the owners were away and having had to dismantle the nest, soft-hearted person that he was, he had no option but to call on us. With only a hint of stumpy feathers showing through the fragile pink skin and its eyes tightly closed, Ma accepted the challenge.

With vigilant twenty-four-hour care, in time its eyes opened, proper plumage grew and most of all, it found a voice. So vocal was the little sparrow (we soon realised what breed it was) that we named it Tweetie. Every day it gained in strength, reacting to Ma's voice by cheeping, and rather than leave it alone in the house, she began to carry it around either tucked inside her bra or perched on her head, snuggled amongst her curls.

Tweetie needed to learn how to fly and Ma took on the role of coach. My brothers and I stood watching this strange performance some distance away, whilst she crouched on the lawn having placed the fledgling on the grass. Walking backwards and flapping her arms, she hoped that Tweetie would follow her. It seemed a fruitless exercise until, on the third day, with more energetic arm waving and encouraging noises, Tweetie took to the air.

The little bird remained Ma's constant companion, following her around the house or in the garden, inches away as she knelt to weed or sow seeds. One afternoon amongst the tomatoes, Ma disturbed an ants' nest, revealing a mass of eggs. Tweetie gorged on the unexpected treats but later when Ma went into the kitchen to wash up after supper, there was no welcoming chirrup and tragically, Tweetie died during the night.

Notes from My Diary

Today, the first of February, the birds are singing, rain has given way to tentative, watery sunshine and with no frost on the grass or ice on the car windscreen, the worst of the winter is behind us. The garden has become a safari park and from the kitchen window over the ensuing hour I counted seven blackbirds, goldfinches, blue and great tits, sparrows, a solitary pied wagtail, two squirrels, a greater spotted woodpecker, greenfinches, chaffinches, a fleet of fat pigeons cruising up the lawn like battleships in formation, a wren scuttling out from underneath a large terracotta tub, a pair of robins, a nuthatch who was struggling to get at the remaining peanuts and joy of joys, a song thrush.

April in full spate and Easter on the horizon, spring has definitely sprung and, as I walk around the garden I am accompanied by the *cheep-cheep-cheep* of baby birds in the nest boxes, fledglings lined up on the washing line, perching in the apple and plum trees and on the terrace, waiting to be fed by their exhausted parents. One blackbird father is becoming increasingly reliant on me to satisfy the demands of his offspring, who turns up his beak to the worms on offer, preferring the sunflower seeds I scatter on the terrace.

So begins an extraordinary story starting last year when a robin family decided to set up home and raise their brood in my kitchen. Such was the unusual if not unique nature of the event, I decided to share it on social media, posting daily bulletins. I had no idea how many people would be caught up in the story as it unfolded, some telling me it was the first thing they looked at when they got up in the morning, brightening the day.

April

Week One

Spot the new guest. This little chap has been visiting the house for the last three days, flying in one morning through my bathroom window and settling on a chair by my bed. Since then, he/she has been coming and going from room to room with no apparent fear.

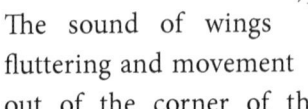

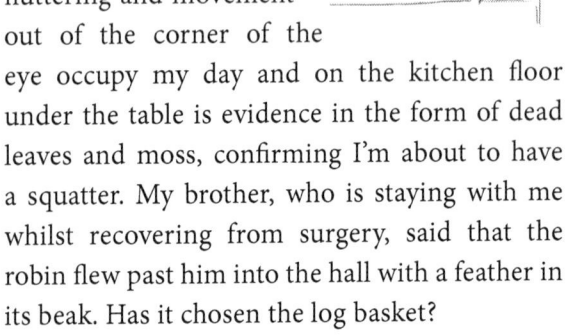

The sound of wings fluttering and movement out of the corner of the eye occupy my day and on the kitchen floor under the table is evidence in the form of dead leaves and moss, confirming I'm about to have a squatter. My brother, who is staying with me whilst recovering from surgery, said that the robin flew past him into the hall with a feather in its beak. Has it chosen the log basket?

The log basket is no longer a contender since I have found out where our friend is setting up home: behind one of the large blue-and-white platters on the pine shelf in the kitchen. Whilst my prospective tenant was out of the room, I carefully removed the dish and saw the beginnings of a des res. Note to self: I'm going to have to leave a window open.

I fixed my telephoto lens to my camera and sat in wait at the kitchen table. Within two minutes, a robin appeared with a mouthful of moss and proceeded to scuffle and scratch on the shelf behind a Nanking and old willow-pattern plate, posing mid-task for a close-up.

Today the construction site has now moved to the left-hand side of the shelf unit. Totally devoid of fear when I click my camera, the robin fixes me with its bright, black eyes, completely motionless and unruffled even though I am not more than eighteen inches away. Amazing.

I've been researching online, which states that one should never go looking for the nest. If you do, more than likely it will be abandoned once they realise its location has been discovered. Obviously, my robins didn't read the memo when they chose my kitchen to raise a brood. I am moved by the enormous faith and confidence this wild creature is extending to me. Further reading informed me of the following facts:

- It is the female who makes the nest, a process which can take two to six days.
- She then has a week off building herself up.
- She will lay an egg a day until there is approximately a clutch of four.
- She will not necessarily stay in the nest during the day and may roost overnight in a tree or shrub.
- Once all the eggs have been laid, she will remain almost constantly on the nest for up to a fortnight, going outside to drink, be fed by her other half or mate in preparation for a second brood.
- Once hatched, both parents will feed the chicks. (This could be fun since I don't know if Mr R has been given a forwarding address.)
- The chicks fledge when twelve to fourteen days old but remain flightless for a further few days.

It seems that about 70% of robins die in the first year from lack of food, exceptionally cold weather, poison or predators and if they survive these perils the average life expectancy can be two to five years although some have been recorded as living as long as ten, even seventeen years. In order to protect the species, the female robin generally has two broods per annum and occasionally four, raising the young from late winter/early spring into the summer months.

Robins tend not to mate for life, but the couple remains together during the breeding season, relying on each other for joint parental duties. It looks as though am I heading for a busy time as I shall be on maternal leave for at least the next five to six weeks.

Week Two

The activity has increased over the last few days and Mrs R is leaving her foraged material along the length of the dresser behind the meat platters. Some heavy lifting is involved and a leaf (at least four times larger than herself) was understandably abandoned and the house is littered with other bits of dried grass and leaves, which haven't made it to the nest, plus droppings. I don't mind a jot.

When I arrived back from shopping this morning, I was greeted by a cheeky face at the kitchen window a beakful of moss giving the impression of a magnificent handlebar moustache. Busy, busy, busy…

I can finally confirm the location for the nest is at the opposite end of the shelf unit from where it all started ten days ago, adjacent to the door to the inner hall and next to the broom cupboard. Footfall and traffic will be a worry for me if not the mum-to-be, but Mrs R is on the nest, seemingly without a care in the world. This means that I shall be able to watch her progress with the next stage – egg laying – from the kitchen table.

18 April

Mrs R doesn't have to travel far to fetch the finishing touches to the nursery as she finds a plentiful supply of moss on the terrace. Job done, she flew inches away from my face, back to the nest.

19 April

Country Life magazine published my letter. Today Hurstpierpoint, tomorrow the world. Mrs R is spending longer periods on the nest. Will she soon start laying?

22 April

Week Three

News Flash!

How do you like your eggs in the morning? In a robin's nest, *oeuf* course. The first perfect cream-coloured, lightly speckled egg has arrived. I wonder how many more will this clever girl lay?

23 April

After only one visit from Mrs R first thing yesterday morning with yet more moss, I was concerned that she might have abandoned the project. However, within the last half hour she is back sitting on the nest, hopefully producing egg number two.

My desk in the office is positioned under a window and a mature shrub in full flower (*viburnum bodnantense*) is outside. It is a haven for sparrows, blue tits and wrens the former nesting under the eaves above. Other visitors are Britain's smallest bird, the gold crest, which cling to the leaded windowpanes in order to gather cobwebs to line their own nests.

24 April
Egg number two has arrived.

25 April
No flying visits today but Mrs R should be back to lay at least one, if not two, more eggs over the course of the next few days. Apparently, no harm comes to them if they are left unattended, which can be as long as two weeks.

Mrs R was absent all day yesterday but this morning, with the return of glorious sunshine, she is back in the kitchen. I am more thrilled than you could possibly imagine.

She's done it! Egg number three has joined the other two.

After successfully laying a third egg this morning, followed by her absence for most of the day, madam is back. Is she laying a fourth? If she has completed the clutch, she will remain on the eggs for twelve to fourteen days until they hatch. This means that I can safely shut the window at night, keeping her – and me – safe.

Yesterday, whilst I was eating my lunch, I was serenaded by my friendly robin companion. Perched on a branch of the crab apple tree in full blossom, it sang its full repertoire, the purest of sounds.

26 April

Mrs R spent the night on the nest and when I went down to the kitchen around 5:00am I opened the window to let her out.

And now there are four.

This morning, when I was sitting in the sunroom, I watched a pair of adult robins outside the window, one feeding the other. I have bought a bag of dried mealworms and have placed some in a small dish by the kitchen window, which was spotted within minutes. Mrs R has been in and out of the kitchen all day and coped fearlessly with the presence of a couple of friends who dropped by, helping herself frequently to these treats, much to their astonishment.

Last night, as the sun was setting, I was washing up my supper dishes when my little robin flew past my shoulder into the garden. As darkness was falling, a robin started to sing in the crab apple tree. I have read that they often sing at night either to expend excess energy, announce their territory, attract a mate, or indicate where there is a source of food. Minutes later, Mrs R flew down from the tree to eat some of the mealworms before returning to the nest to bed down for the night.

Madam has taken a lunch break al fresco and had a good drink from Jess's (my rescue Labrador) water bowl, followed by a bath and preen before returning to the kitchen to feast on mealworms. All good. All happy.

Week Four

28 April

Exciting development this morning. I have been concerned about Mr R and his forthcoming duties in caring for the young when they hatch. How will he know where the nest is? He might not have visited the kitchen or anywhere else in the house and wouldn't have a clue what to do. However, this morning while I was having a coffee with an old school friend on her way down to see her brother in Cooden, we heard a series of tiny, high-pitched squeaks followed by a similar response from the garden. I am sure it was the two parents who were touching base and possibly passing on information.

30 April

Another peaceful night and I was greeted by a blue tit flying about in the kitchen. Obviously, the word is out: 'AirBirdnB/Des Res available: one bed apartment on the ground floor with restaurant and twenty-four hour concierge. Apply within….'

May

1 May

Had a minor panic this morning when I found the nest was empty, but last night when I shut the window, I wasn't sure if Mrs R was safely inside, or had I shut her out? I opened the window in case and immediately she flew in, landed on the kettle, followed by the tap and now is back on the eggs.

Just experienced a very, very special moment. I was at the sink (my 'studio') painting a vase of roses and vibrant lime-green lady's mantle arranged in a crystal vase when Mrs R landed inches away from me. Instead of flying off, she hopped into the dish provided and proceeded to have her fill of mealworms, some grated cheese and other tasty morsels for a good two minutes before flying back to the nest. I talked to her while she was eating and when she lifted her head, she looked me straight in the eye as though listening to me.

3 May

Magic garden fairy Jess (she of two feet, not four) is busy in the borders and a robin came to help. Was it Mrs R or the other half? I checked the nest in the kitchen, and it was empty, so the jury is out. Minutes later, I saw two robins on the gate by the kitchen, one feeding the other.

Looks like I am in for the long haul. According to the internet, it takes the babies about a fortnight to leave the nest and then they stay with their parents for a further two or three weeks. The father continues to feed them while the mother starts incubating a new brood of eggs in another nest close by.

5 May
This is Mr R. How do I know this? Because, if you look closely, you can see that he has a bright green caterpillar in his beak and has come to feed his girl who, while devouring mealworms, was watching him from the kitchen window before they both flew off together.

Week Five

6 May
Coronation Day

It has been very difficult to concentrate on the extraordinary ceremony in Westminster Abbey with what is going on in the garden. Mrs R uttered her first squeaks of the day from the safety of the nest and within seconds Mr R appeared on the bird bath. Calling out again, she left the nest to join him outside. Flying onto the lawn, he set to work and found a worm, which he promptly fed to her before she rushed back to her eggs. Then, there was another fluttering of wings and a wren appeared with a beak full of leaves by a tiny nest box attached to a climbing rose on the arbour. I watched fascinated as he (for it is the male who makes the nest) is going backwards and forwards with more material.

I won't get anything done today with all these distractions. Mr R has been back with another caterpillar and although he called to Mrs R and even sang to her with the grub in his beak, she remained on her eggs, so he ate it. Mr Wren, on the other hand, is constructing the nest in record time. Apparently, they build up to three nests and then invite the female to inspect each of them before she decides which one she prefers, abandoning the others.

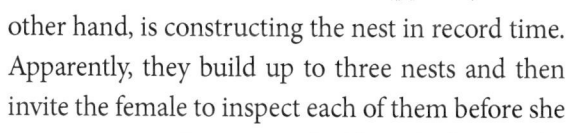

7 May

It can't be long now before the chicks emerge. Will it be on Tuesday? Wednesday? Mrs R has popped out for a mid-morning feed, her high-pitched squeaks reassuring Mr R, who is never far away, that she was about to appear and straight away he landed on one of the chairs to feed her. The first delicacy down the hatch, he flew off only to return seconds later with another. I am loving this.

8 May

We have lift-*oeuf*! Two of the eggs have hatched – but I don't want to get too close in case I frighten them. This is perhaps the most exciting thing to have happened to me in years. We have a new king and a new family of baby robins. What a start to the week.

The toings and froings are increasing by the minute with very close and personal fly-pasts skimming over my shoulder before landing on the edge of the pine shelf to feed a still-silent brood. Angela, friend from next door, called by and was worried her presence would upset them. Upset? Nah! Each time one of the parents flew into the kitchen it paused either on the back of a chair, the floor or any other suitable landing place within less than three feet of us. Angela watched, transfixed. I don't think she really believed me when I told her what was going on but now, having seen it for herself, she was astounded. The last of the four eggs must have hatched because we watched Mrs R eating an

empty shell before settling
back on her babies. I am
truly besotted.

9 May

Breakfast time. Mrs R flew past
me as I was slicing a piece of bread. So far,
I can only spot two little
yellow beaks.

I can see three little
beaks.

10 May

The live mealworms
have arrived in the
post, and it took Mrs R a matter of
seconds before she spotted
them wriggling on the dish. I
had to work fast as she took
the first one on the wing.
I think the chicks are
going to love them,
although I'm not
so sure that I
shall be too happy
keeping them in
the fridge.

11 May

I'm pretty sure I can now identify which little bird is which: Mr R is the one on the left, feeding his girl, but if they weren't together, I would know it was him because his tummy feathers are uniformly grey, whereas Mrs R has much darker markings. Now I can check to see if he is doing what he ought to in helping to feed the babies.

It's 9:15pm and normally Mrs R is tucked up on the nest. However, she hasn't returned from the garden and it's pitch-black outside. I must close the window and turn off the lights but fear that I shall be shutting her outside. In a turmoil not knowing what to do I googled 'does the robin sleep on the nest with the chicks at night?' and the answer is 'yes', for the first few days and then she leaves them alone unless the temperature drops. If she hasn't come back within the next five to ten minutes, I shall put the house to bed.

12 May

Last night I was worried about Mrs R being away from the nest but when I checked later this morning, she was back. I am going to contact the RSPB today to see if they can give me any more information about what the next week or so will hold. Mrs R will probably leave her young soon at night, returning at daybreak to feed them but I want to make sure I do the right thing. In the meantime, the remaining mealworms have disappeared in the brief time I was upstairs.

I emailed the RSPB:

'I wonder if you could please give me some advice. I have a robin nesting in my kitchen. Three chicks hatched out of four eggs on Monday, and all is going very well, with both parents feeding them caterpillars, etc. from the garden and live mealworms I purchased from a reputable supplier. I read online that, after a few days, the chicks are left alone in the nest while the parents sleep elsewhere. My conundrum is this: when does this nocturnal separation commence?'

Mrs R wasn't on the nest at 9:15pm. Fifteen

minutes later, she flew in, and I could go to bed.
Had an informative telephone chat with a very helpful person at the RSPB and she confirmed that it is likely Mrs R will begin to sleep away from her babies at night. Apparently, robins fledge quickly and there should be signs of a departure within the next eight to ten days. In the meantime, I'm going to rig up a platform or something to catch them should they drop or fall out of the nest, which is a good three to four feet off the ground. When they do eventually fledge, Mr R will take the parental baton while Mrs R searches out a new location nearby in preparation for another brood. The next few weeks will be busy and thank goodness I have no plans to go away.

Now, when the chicks are being fed, they utter the tiniest little chirruping noise. Two push their way to the front while number three is always late to the party when Mum arrives with the next meal. Still no sign of number four. I would think their eyes will open any day and stubbly feathers should soon break through. Earlier today I saw Mrs R fly away from the nest with a something small and white in her beak. It was one of the chick's poo. The nest is kept immaculately clean and when one of the babies wants to go to the loo, it up-ends its bottom like a duck diving on a pond, followed by the expulsion of a little sack containing the gubbins for the parent to pluck away before discarding it in the garden. Clever stuff.

The honeymoon is not over, and parenthood has not brought about headaches or undue tiredness to the parents, because five minutes ago when I was washing up, Mrs R flew out of the window, had a sip of water from the rain-filled trug before landing on the back of a chair and starting to sing. Within a split second, Mr R appeared, fed her a titbit, flew off, then came back for them to mate. What a pair.

A final post before bedtime. Mr R is in the young oak tree singing his valiant heart out in harmony with a male blackbird perched on the chimney. A perfect evensong.

13 May

Mrs R was tucked up in the kitchen last night when I returned from shutting up the chickens. I have three girls: all gentle, chatty souls but one seems to have a particular fondness for me and when I go to shut the pop-hole door, two are safely inside the coop but number three remains outside. She runs towards me, wings outstretched and squats on her hunkers waiting for me to pick her up for a cuddle and possibly a bedtime story.

Week Six

14 May

Yesterday, after an early morning visit from my feathered friends, things went very quiet, and I didn't catch sight of either robin again all day. I feared the worst, but all was back to normal later in the day. This morning it seems as though there might only be two little birds unless the third chick keeps himself to himself behind the dinner plate. Mr R arrived a few moments ago with breakfast but, not as bold as Mrs R, was reluctant to come into the kitchen, having spotted me reading the paper. I left the room to give him space and instantly he went to his babies. Tiny stumps of emerging feathers are appearing, and their eyes are open.

It's 9:40pm and three little babies are sound asleep. There is no sign of Mrs R. However, as I was filling my hottie, she flew past me to the nest then back outside. I waited over half an hour, and she hadn't returned so I ran the gauntlet and shut the window.

15 May

I worried all night about my charges being left without their mummy. This morning, they were still asleep, a poo sack perched on the edge of the nest. I have just had another peep; the poo has gone, and three wide-open beaks greeted me. Still no sign of number four. Mrs R is back. Already a week old, their stubbly feathers are growing at the rate of knots.

15 May

Motherhood, albeit by default, is not without jeopardy and since waking this morning at 4:00am I dreaded what I might find. However, great news: it's just gone 7:00am and I was greeted by a chorus of cheeping coming from three expectant beaks. Going to the sink to fill the kettle, one of the robins flew past me to feed the brood before settling down in the nest. The timing was perfect, or was it fate that I happened to be in the right place at the right time to open the window, unless the parents were watching outside for this to happen?

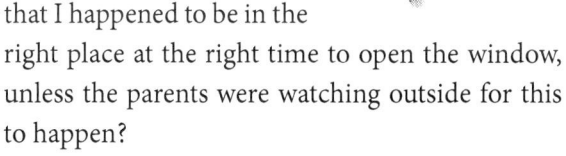

I have decided to forego the live mealworms, giving them to the birds in the garden. I think they were too big for little beaks, so I've gone back to the smaller, dried mealworms. Also, they have a tendency to crawl out of the dish onto the work surface…

The kitchen has become like the M25 in rush hour.

The activity has definitely pegged up a gear or three with one parent immediately following the other, beaks charged with caterpillars and insects. The chicks are getting bigger by the day, and I am concerned that with all the wriggling to be fed first they risk falling. When there was a very brief hiatus in the feeding rota, I managed to rig up a small open cardboard box tucked in the shelf below so if any of the chicks does come a cropper, hopefully it would land safely enabling me to put it back with no harm done. They have another week or less to go before they fledge, in which time they will probably double in size and this will present a real worry for Mr and Mrs R, not least me.

On another note, I made myself an asparagus/leek cheesy flan for supper – a bit like a quiche without the pastry and when I put a slice on a plate, Mr R appeared at the window. Still slightly apprehensive about coming into the house with me so close, I moved a discreet distance away. He quickly fed the babies, to much chattering and chirping, and then landed on the edge of the dish in which I had cooked my supper gobbling up crumbs of grated Gruyère.

A most extraordinary ending to the day when I discovered that there are four thriving chicks, not three. Having risked moving the meat platter to give more space on the narrow shelf, number four (who had been hiding at the back) is now clearly in the running at mealtimes. I am so thrilled that the clever little mum has hatched every single egg. What a girl!

16 May

The last few hours have been very worrying, when my fears were confirmed yesterday evening: one of the chicks had fallen from the nest and in spite of the pile of cushions on top of the table, somehow it had tumbled to the floor. Carefully, I picked up the little mite, less than a couple of inches long, and placed it tenderly back in the nest. I worried all night, fearing what I might find this morning. Again, there was a chick on the cushions, still breathing, thank goodness. Whether or not it was the same baby there is no way of knowing. There were three tiny sacks of poo on the rim of the nest, which I removed with tweezers, proving hopefully that the other three nestlings were okay. The window is wide open, dawn is about to break, and I pray that Mr and Mrs R return to the nursery. It is hard to believe that something so tiny and helpless which would fit in a matchbox will be able, almost, to fend for itself in a matter of days.

It's 7:00am and both parents are back on duty and four little yellow beaks clamour for food. I shall be watching even more closely from now on.

After rescuing the fledglings twice overnight, it happened a third time this morning, the cushions providing a soft landing. None the worse for wear, the nest is back to a full quota. Confident that the tumbles were caused by lack of space, over-enthusiastic jostling for food and not a death wish, I went shopping. They are now eagerly waiting the next meal – unless further escapees need my help. Motherhood is exhausting.

I don't know if I can stand the excitement – and I hope I am not boring everyone with this saga. Going into the kitchen to check all was well, Mr R was on the tiled floor. When Jess and I walked past him, he was totally unperturbed and flew up to his babies before dive bombing me (I had to duck to avoid being crashed into) on his way back into the garden. He is becoming much bolder and used to my presence so much so that when I was reading the paper on the terrace, twice he settled on the back of a chair opposite me with a beak full of grubs. It was almost as though he was showing me what a good daddy he is. Once he's fed the gang – they are on the fresh food – he goes for the dried mealworms, the takeaway option. The more I watch the bird activity in the garden, the more I realise how awful and unnecessary pesticides are – the avian community does a cracking job in controlling things.

Should a paint manufacturer need inspiration for a new shade of yellow, might I suggest Baby Robin's Beak?

What a difference a day makes. Their feathers are growing in leaps and bounds. I love the fluffiest of baby down on their heads – every mother's nightmare when getting dressed for school.

Oops! I turn my back for one split second… Back into the nest you go, little scallywag.

Forget the M25 at rush hour – it's turned into Piccadilly Circus/Hyde Park Corner and Spaghetti Junction rolled into one.

A table for two? Lunch al sinko with Mr R. We split the bill.

All my ducks, sorry, chicks in a row, who don't look as though falling from the nest has caused any long-term harm.

17 May

It's coming up to 5:00am and I woke later than normal, relaxed in the knowledge that I had done all I possibly could to keep my young guests safe overnight. The mother of invention is necessity, as my old prep schoolteacher Miss Wiles used to say. I shall explain. I had been deliberating and pondering the best method to secure the baby birds in the nest and then had a light-bulb moment. Robins nest in an open-fronted box or location rather than an enclosed one. Why not use a stiff-picture mount? The card is light and easily attached with masking tape to the wooden frame of the shelf and has an aperture large enough to give air but with a sufficiently wide brim to prevent a tumble. It worked a dream. The babies were still sleeping when I peeled it back and within five minutes of opening the window, the parents were back on duty, first removing any poo sacks before beginning the relentless feeding.

Being able to observe the robins' activity, it's interesting to note that the insects, grubs, etc.

which are being offered to the four babies are increasing in size, the worms considerably larger than those of a few days ago.

18 May

Good morning! It's just gone 5:15am and my babies are sleepy but rousing, with the exception of number four who, as per usual is conspicuous by its absence, preferring to remain a-bed behind the meat plate.

My dear Mr R is looking more and more bedraggled. Although Mrs R is very much on-duty, it seems to be the daddy doing most of the work. This will continue big time when the Robinets (a suggested name for them) quit home, as he will be the sole carer for a couple of weeks before they can fend for themselves. My heart goes out to the parents, and I'm tempted to give them the local number for Deliverobin or Worms R Us in the hope that they get a bit of time off.

One worry: the dish with the mealworms was empty when I came downstairs this morning. Also, the container with Jess's treats was on its side, having been tipped over. Far too heavy to be the work of the robins, I'm scared that it might be caused by magpies. I have now hidden the mealworms out of sight, but I shall keep an extra vigilant eye in case I'm right, my main fear being they spot where the nest is.

19 May

Mrs R, who has been on a short break, reappeared this morning on full feeding frenzy but looking fagged out like many a new mum. She is stocking up on the dried mealworms each time she has deposited the worms or insects in ever-demanding beaks, passing mid-air above the sink with Mr R as he flies in.

There has been a massive growth spurt in the last twenty-four hours and the babies are now twice the size, stacked on top of each other like loaves of sliced bread on a shelf in the supermarket.

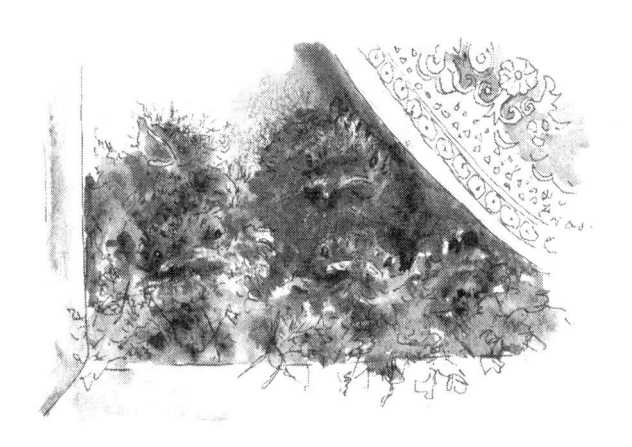

20 May

Tweedledum and Tweedledee have dropped from the nest *again* and are cuddled up on the cushions. I shan't return them to the nest as I feel that they are just about ready to go into the outside world. However, I shall wait until the other two join them before taking the plunge. I am sure that the parents will be able to look after them in the meantime, feeding them as usual. I shall be on hand virtually all morning, if not all day to make sure that all proceeds to plan and no accidents occur.

Mr R is on nappy duty, removing the poo sack from one of the chicks. He looks smaller but it is a trick of the light; they are still fluffy, feathery balls of baby bird. Having dealt with one chick, he waited patiently for any more sacks of poo to emerge before despatching them.

'Feed me! Feed me!'

I am still not sure if the first two chicks deliberately left the nest at dawn or whether they fell. I shall be more certain of the former if they are followed later by their siblings. However, they are still vulnerable, and I am faced with this conundrum: should I now release them into the garden? I won't return them to the nest as they are too large to fit in the small space. Oh, the worry of doing the right/wrong thing... The bad news is that a magpie landed on the kitchen windowsill.

I hope I don't have further cause for concern. There is a lot of high-pitched squeaking and communication between Mr and Mrs R and this last visit made me worry as Mr R remained by the nest for much longer than a fleeting visit.

There was no happy chirruping from the chicks, and he seemed to be listening and waiting for them to react. When he left, I checked to see if they were alive, and they are breathing. So am I.

All is well at base camp. Mr R consumes some mealworms before returning to the nest to feed the babies with the freeze-dried insects. This is the first time I have seen the babies being given these rather than live worms and small grubs. I shall have to buy some more as they have now all been eaten. I can almost hear the two mischief makers saying, 'Oi, Dad, come back. That didn't hit the sides!'.

Worried that the escapees weren't getting the attention they need, I grasped the nettle and put them back in the nest and now the naughty pair are being fed, possibly at the expense of the others.

I dropped some mozzarella on the work surface and Mr R picked it up and flew off. Mealworms are never going to taste as good.

Mishi Bellamy, a friend, suggested hanging a bird scarer and I remember having made such a thing years ago to stop the jackdaws flying into the chicken run. All you need is a large potato, some feathers, string and a skewer. This took two minutes to cobble together and it's hovering realistically. Let's hope the magpies and jays haven't been to Specsavers and that it doesn't frighten the robins into the bargain.

Week Seven

21 May

Sunday morning – could this be the day my babies depart good 'n' proper? They have tripled in size over the last two weeks and are really cramped for space. I'm not going anywhere.

I'm not sure what is happening. When I came down this morning there were four chubby little nestlings and straight away, when I opened the window, Mr R was back on feeding and nappy duty. However, at about 7:30am I heard the magpie outside and rushed downstairs and now it looks as though there might only be three in the nest. I searched everywhere to see if the fourth had fallen to the floor and was hiding but there was only a trace of poo on the tiles and another on the lid of a jar by the sink. I waited to see if I could spot the possible culprit but to no avail. Mr R reappeared and went to feed the babies but there was no chirruping on this or subsequent visits, and it looks sadly as though one has disappeared. Did a magpie come into the kitchen and if so, did it take one of the babies? There is no sign of entry or a tussle, but I can only assume that this is what might have happened and why the chicks are silent. If this is the case, the bird will be back. I don't know what to do.

21 May
I have just heard scuffling behind a box on the floor where I keep my paints and art equipment and there was the fledgling. However, it moved too fast, and I couldn't catch it but at least I know it's safe – for the moment. Mr R is on the window squeaking as I am sure he knows one of his babies needs him. I am a wreck.

Number one is safely secured in a cardboard box until I know what to do next. Mr R is in the kitchen watching the proceedings and he knows where this offspring is judging by the squawks and fluttering coming from inside the box. I reckon this one will be the first to fly as it's a feisty little fellow and if any of them survives my money is on him.

In every good story there should be conflict but in this case, I could do with a smooth run. In the hope of avoiding further incident to avoid possible disaster when the remaining nestlings emerge, I have placed a cardboard box on the cushions beneath, which should catch them when they fall. At least I can go and get dressed in the knowledge that they won't land on the floor. My hair will turn completely white with the stress.

21 May

In my absence walking Jess, it looks like number two has left the nest but where is it? Mr R is squeaking constantly and continues to feed the remaining pair. Is he trying to encourage the babies to join him? I shan't be able to move from the kitchen. It's going to be a long day

Number one was getting more and more agitated doing jumping jacks in the box which I had placed next to the nest. The good news is that after searching in every nook and cranny in the kitchen for number two, I spotted it on the shelf behind another meat dish. I felt I had no option other than to gather all the chicks and carry them into the garden. Instantly, three of them hopped out, the fourth remaining in the box and within seconds, Mr or Mrs R appeared. They know they are there, and I am sure will lead them to safety.

Something extraordinary took place. I saw Mr and Mrs R disappear several times in the corner where the hostas are, hopefully having gathered up the young. However, one of the parents landed on the window and remained there for over five minutes, if not longer, chattering as though talking to me. I am sure it wasn't searching for the chicks but letting me know that he was grateful for my help – or that's what I chose to think.

I'm pretty certain I know where the robin family has set up home and I shall now leave them in peace at this very new and challenging time. Having said that, the contact isn't totally over as Mr R is still coming into the kitchen to feast on the dish of mealworms, both for him and his growing family.

It is with a huge sigh of relief that I can say with confidence that both Mr and Mrs R are busy caring for their young in the great outdoors. I saw the two of them greeting each other on the wing before Mr R came for his mealworms. I was having my lunch (freshly picked asparagus, lettuce and radishes) and he joined me every couple of minutes. I added some crumbs of cheese to his mix, and this was wolfed down in a trice. I now have to include Davidstow special vintage Cheddar to my shopping list to keep the boy happy.

I have a feeling that my little family has relocated to the side of the house where I store unused pots and where, ahem, the weeds have taken over. Very quietly, with neither parent in sight, I had a sneaky peek and there, on an old hanging basket on the ground, was one of the fledglings, then I saw one of the parents waiting nearby to feed them It's the perfect spot: sheltered, no one walks past (including Jess) and with plenty of ground cover for protection.

22 May

I try not to think too much about my charges and how they might have coped with their first night away from home. Although I had visits yesterday from Mr R, who continues to enjoy the mealworms, so far this morning there has been neither sight nor sound. I am anxious beyond words.

I feared that my unorthodox act of liberating the fledglings myself instead of letting nature take its course was putting at risk all the hard work both Mr and Mrs R and I had put in to raise the young. However, thanks to Frank Wilson, who reassured me that the little ones will tuck themselves away safely out of sight in the knowledge that their parents will know where they are, I am reassured that my actions might have been correct.

I had to go shopping, which meant shutting the kitchen windows but before I locked up, I put a handful of mealworms on the sill outside. On driving down the lane two minutes from home, something truly magical happened. In the middle of the road was a deer with a faun and what looked like a very large rabbit or hare. I have never seen a hare in Sussex although I am sure they live on the Downs. Then, all three animals started to walk very slowly together to the other side of the lane, and I realised that they were in fact two fauns with their mother. The smaller of the two was paler grey with a slightly mottled coat and I don't think could have been more than a few hours or days old at the most. I drove by carefully in case they stepped onto the road and then heard squeaks. I stopped the car and walked back and there, in the long grass, was the tiny baby. It looked at me, stood up and joined its mother and sibling through a large gap in the hedge. Honestly and truly, with everything going on in my life, I feel more and more like Snow White.

Back to my robins: having opened the kitchen window, I started to give homes to my shopping when I noticed that the pepper mill was on its side. Seconds later, Mr R flew past me into the garden, his beak full of mealworms and dived into the border by the terrace. He must have realised that he couldn't get into the house downstairs and had flown through the only other window open in my bedroom. What a clever, clever boy he is.

Very quietly, when Mr and Mrs

R were off foraging (I could hear their squeaks), as I didn't want the parents to know that I was aware of the location of their babies, I didn't try to seek out the other chicks. The relief that at least one fledgling has survived, if not the others, is immense. I shall now leave them in peace. Oh, happy day.

I've been watching Mr R on top of the window calling out to his chicks, an insect peeking out from his half-open beak. I thought it might have got stuck together at the end but after about three minutes he swallowed it. Then he called out full throttle to his babies, but they haven't answered. I hope all is well.

What an afternoon. Mr R returned to his look-out post on top of the open window and started to squeak. Actually, it was more of a cry, a plea, and he continued this for over fifteen minutes with no response. Nothing. Two friends who had heard about the remarkable happenings arrived and found me standing on the path by the kitchen window, some crumbs of cheese in my hand. Mr R looked at the treats two inches away from his claws and helped himself to a morsel for the first time. Not only that, but he also allowed me to stroke the feathers on his tummy before flying to the rose arch where he continued his plaintive lament. Eventually, after a good half hour, he gathered up some mealworms and disappeared into the border. Then, we heard cheeping. He had located his babies. We spent the next forty minutes watching his trips back and forth from the kitchen to the lawn and then into the undergrowth happy in the knowledge that the family was reunited.

I am convinced that a bird can experience emotion, and this was one very worried father.

Mr R has had a bath. Anything to cool off after the latest worries but Mrs R wasn't there to hold his towel and I have never seen such a scruffy individual when he emerged, feathers all over the place, hair in a mess.

23 May

Another day, another dawn, and after a brief silent hiatus the squeaking has kick-started. I have just spotted Mr R feeding Mrs R on the branch of the malus tree. Then he flew to his favourite spot on the rose arch where I was standing, as if to say, 'good morning!' before heading off for some mealworms. I wonder how many little beaks he is filling. After fledging, the chicks should remain in hiding for a few more days before venturing out and stretching their strengthening wings but no proper arial activity for several days.

It's late afternoon and I heard the terrifying squawks of two magpies heading for the kitchen window. I yelled and screamed at them, which didn't stop Mr R from squeaking. Now all is silent.

24 May

A friend who had come to spend the night saw one of the magpies divebomb the kitchen window. We thought it was going for Mr R but in fact, it was simply the irresistible lure of free food. I closed the window, hid the mealworms and we carried on chatting. Five minutes later, there was a whirring of wings coming from the door to the hall and Mr R flew past us towards the window, which remained closed to prevent further magpie action. He had an insect in his beak and, taking a second or two to register the problem, escaped through the open door to the garden. Once again, he had found the bedroom window open. We were astonished at the intelligence of such a tiny creature.

26 May

All has been relatively quiet on the robin front, although Mr R remains a regular visitor. He has now raised the bar to grated vintage parmesan. When I was washing a lettuce a fat slug slid out, which I placed in the mealworm dish. Mr R must have eyes in the back of his head because quicker than a flash, he snaffled it.

I wrote to *Country Life* giving them an update:

Nest place

FURTHER to my published missive (*Letters, April 19*) concerning the family of robins nesting in my kitchen, I thought you might like to receive a happy update: all four eggs hatched and they are thriving.
Bryony Hill, West Sussex

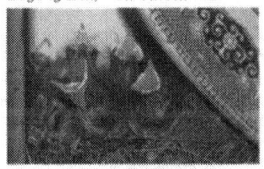

Country Life, 24 May 2023

I bought some Cornish new potatoes from Rhubarb Greengrocer in the village this morning and they knocked spots off the Jersey Royals for flavour. Nibbling at one straight from the saucepan, I watched as Mr R landed on the window sill. Putting a small piece of potato in the palm of my hand, he hopped over (all of two inches) and took it.

27 May

I am learning so much about robins. This morning, I called in to the pet shop in the village to get some more mealworms as I felt a diet of cheese and potato wasn't quite pukka tukka. Andrée was a mine of information and told me that Mr R is eating all he can to build up his strength, hence his continued visits to the kitchen whilst feeding his young solely on live insects, grubs and caterpillars. As I feared, the dried food/cheese isn't suitable. We are coming up to a week since the four chicks left the nest.

Week Eight

28 May

Mel came to lunch yesterday and we set up in the shade on the terrace halfway between the stash of mealworms by the window and where Mr R is keeping his brood safely in the bushes and undergrowth. I wanted to see if he was confident enough in Mel's presence to eat from my hand and in anticipation, I picked off a small piece of brie (Somerset – no air miles) but although he had spotted it from his launch pad in the flowering cherry tree, he didn't seem all that interested. However, when I took some plates back to the kitchen, Mr R landed on the back of my chair and then grabbed the morsel of cheese from the table. He seems to be totally at ease with anyone and everyone and, of course, he is on a mission.

29 May

The word is about. The avian Tripadvisor network

has spread the news that the twenty-four/seven takeaway feeding station is open to all and sundry and there is now a pair of blackbirds vying for pickings outside the kitchen window. I know they love sultanas and raisins, and I shall put a few out but well beyond reach of Jess as they are toxic to dogs.

Had to call into the chemist this morning to pick up my meds and chatted to a friend while we were waiting to be served. The first thing she asked me was, 'how are the robins?'.

She is not on Facebook but knew all about my house guests and then the next person in the queue said, 'you're Bryony, aren't you? I've heard all about your robins too and am loving the story!'.

Hey, we've gone viral.

2 June

It is now nearly two weeks since I released the robin family into the garden. Mr R continues raiding his own personal sushi bar, now liberally embellished with dried shrimp and other insects so maybe, just maybe, the fledglings will come out into the open.

3 June

Whilst watering the pots outside the kitchen, Mr R pitched up for a lunchtime snack. I was perfectly positioned to see if he is continuing to feed his brood in their hiding place under the tree peony and lilac and, yes, sure enough, he is. It's now nearly two weeks since I helped them fledge from the kitchen and set them free. I wonder if Mrs R has installed herself on a new nest? If so, her latest clutch of eggs should be on the verge of hatching. This will mean that Mr R has time for her and, when she leaves the nest for a quick drink, I might catch him feeding her again. My camera is ever ready.

Week Ten

4 June

Whilst patiently scrubbing some new potatoes which I shall steam on a bed of apple mint, Mr R popped in for an early evening snack. He watched quizzically as I scraped away, kicking the mealworms, dried insects and tiny shrimp onto the work surface before selecting one which appealed more than the others. Off he flew without a backward glance to feed his offspring who have quit base camp beneath the tree peony and are now installed at second base under or near the acer.

6 June

I am so excited. Mr R has continued his frequent visits to the feeding trough in the kitchen and I have been entertained by the constant cheeping of a family of blue tits about to flee the nest by the terrace, matched by fresh squeaks coming from where my robin(s) are secreted. Then all of a sudden, whilst reading the final pages of Rory Knight Bruce's delightful autobiography, a baby robin landed on the back of the chair opposite me. Then he flew into the nearby malus just as Mr R arrived to feed him, giving me so much hope that at least one of the four chicks has survived.

7 June

Sitting for a quiet moment reading today's *Country Life* (no letter from me this week), a juvenile robin landed on the edge of the fountain and was having a drink. Then it decided to have its first bath. With lots of splashing about, it flew off only to return seconds later, no doubt having been told by its parents to go back and wash behind its ears. Obeying the powers that be, I was witness to further splashing and preening.

Thanks to my robins making so much noise, I know when something is going on. The latest outburst was a serious cry for attention. I have come to the conclusion that only this individual has survived, and I reckon it must be the first baby who relentlessly escaped from the nest in the kitchen and was first out of the cardboard box when I released them in the garden.

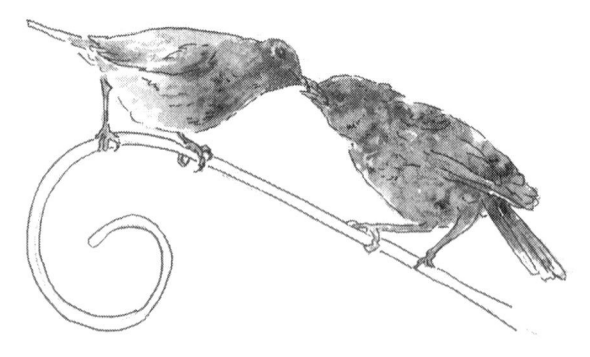

8 June
What an obliging pair they are. I only have to go into the garden and there they are, Mr R and chick, the latter nearly the same size as dad.

10 June
I feel I have reached the point where I can close the final chapter on what has been one of the most endearing experiences of my life. Mr R came to feed in the kitchen yesterday evening and spent quite a while eating while I prepared my supper. Today, he has remained distant until he took a bath near where I was sitting on the terrace under the rose arbour. There is no sign of the fledgling and hopefully he/she is living independently. Mrs R no doubt is incubating another clutch of eggs, therefore Mr R's attentions must be centred in her

direction. I am hoping to catch them meeting up in the garden as they did before. It is with more than a touch of sadness and a feeling of empty-nest syndrome that I write this post but also one filled with satisfaction that there is, after all, a happy ending to this remarkable story.

Week Eleven

11 June

And we thought it was all over. Mr R, having completed his task and left his sole baby to fend for itself, I thought that he would be occupying himself elsewhere and I would be the last thing on his mind. But no. Whilst reading the Sunday papers on the terrace, a tired, hot Jess at my feet, there came a familiar flutter and a flurry and lo and behold, Mr R was back. He hopped from the paving stones onto the lower bar of the bench a couple of feet away and looked at me as though he was saying, 'hello, my friend. I haven't forgotten you'. There followed a moment of amusement when he attempted to perform a vertical take-off onto the top of the dwarf wall but didn't quite make it and, as if to hide his blushes, he flew to the open kitchen window where I continue to keep a dish of goodies.

16 June

My boy still has time for me with several daily visits to have a chat and a snack. Today, he landed on the ground next to me, spent a while looking at me, cocking his head as I spoke to him and then flew up onto the back of the chair. He continued to observe me intently, listening all the while as I chatted before nipping off for some mealworms in the kitchen. My goodness, he's a messy eater!

Week Twelve

18 June

Once Mr R was no longer preoccupied with fatherhood, I thought that our relationship would quietly wind down and these updates would find a natural conclusion. How wrong I was. Mr R continues to visit the kitchen to feed on mealworms and this morning, a robin appeared on top of the gate post. By the lack of a fully developed red breast it wasn't Mr R. Could it be the surviving baby robin I had helped to fledge a month ago? He remained on the post looking at me and listening to me as I spoke to him with no intention of flying away. This lasted a good five minutes during which time he bobbed forwards several times as if about to launch himself in my direction and, in the hope that he might come nearer, I fetched the dish of mealworms and placed it on the table. Straight away he flew down and landed on the back of the chair where he continued to stare, head cocked, beak open and then retreated one leg into his feathered tummy. The leg reappeared and after a good scratch, he jumped down onto the dish and ate mealworm after mealworm. With less than two feet between us, Jess under the table, he was totally relaxed. Replete, he flew into the nearby cherry tree, and I thought that was it for the day but within ten minutes he was back to feed again, diving straight onto the dish with no half-way resting post.

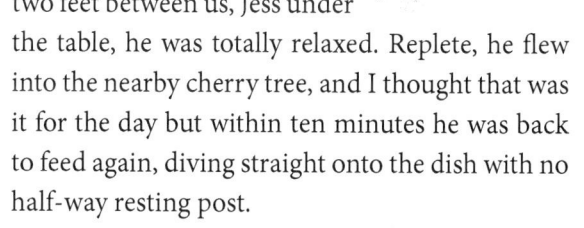

I went to fetch my camera and waited patiently, and before long baby R was back. He took his time before flying down to the dish on the table, but it gave me the chance to take some pictures to see if he was concerned by the camera's click. Not a bit of it, and I took photo after photo, and he didn't blink any eye. What a star!

20 June

As it started to rain, I brought in the dish of mealworms into the kitchen. Our little chap isn't daft and within seconds flew to the window. I went to fetch my camera and he was still there and squeaked when I approached. I took several pictures, getting nearer each time, ending no more than ten inches away from him – and still he didn't fly off.

July

1 July

Remember when I was concerned about fledging the chicks? One of them had a wobbly foot and I'm pretty sure (by looking closely at my new visitor) it is the same robin, as his right 'ankle' is slightly more swollen than the other one. It makes sense that it was this baby who survived as he was the more determined of all of them.

The garden has turned into a bird nursery: the old apple tree was alive with heaven knows how many long-tailed tits, four young kestrels were having raucous fun flying in and out of the giant oak tree, the young magpies which nested on the top of the Japanese maple badgered their parents for food on the lawn, baby blue tits chirruped in the Scots pine and Mr (or was it Mrs?) R paid me a visit, eating some remaining mealworms I had scattered on the table followed by a drink of water. Then, to top it all, when I was walking with Jess around the garden, I spotted a barn owl flying silently over the water meadow.

Epilogue

September

The house was full of men; I was having a new boiler fitted, so I went into the sunroom with Jess to keep out of their way. All of a sudden, Mrs R flew in. She hadn't been in the house since the babies fledged and it was quite a surprise. With Jess sleeping at my feet, she landed first on the television and then on the sofa beside me, where she looked at me with such concentration that I was sure she was trying to tell me something. Dropping onto the carpet, ignoring Jess, she escaped through the open window. This was the last intimate contact we shared for several weeks.

The summer had come and gone, and although I kept a dish of mealworms by the kitchen window, there were few visits from my robins, and I could only assume they were busy elsewhere. However, in November, as the nights were drawing in, Mrs R returned.

The mealworms were being eaten on the windowsill and I was looking forward to renewing our special friendship over the winter months.

11 November

A week later, a noise came from the kitchen, indicating that Mrs R was back. She flew into the hall, then upstairs into my bedroom, perching on my dressing gown hanging on the back of the door, where she allowed me to approach and stroke her tummy before she flew out of the window.

January

A New Year

18 January

I came back from letting out and feeding the chickens to find a welcoming committee in the kitchen: Mrs R. Totally unfazed by my presence or close proximity of Jess when she flew onto the tiles inches from her, she hopped and flew around before returning to the garden. I was more convinced that she was checking out possible nesting places for a new family in a few weeks' time.

February

4 February

My little robin was waiting on the sill by the kitchen window as I walked up the garden with Jess. I unlocked the door and grabbed a handful of mixed seeds and mealworms. Mrs R hopped along, looking at me steadily, before eating out of my hand.

7 February

Oh my! Not one but two robins in the kitchen a minute ago. They are definitely a pair and came to the terrace by the kitchen window waiting to be fed. Showing no fear, I was able to get within a foot or two with a handful of seeds so they could help themselves, which one of them did, from my outstretched hand.

14 February

Valentine's Day. Mr and Mrs R arrived together this morning and flew around the kitchen, stopping here and there before eating mealworms. Love is in the air again.

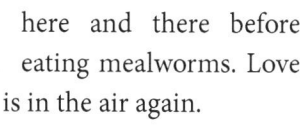

Then a miracle happened. Mrs R came into the kitchen with a large leaf in her beak and flew past me straight to the pine shelf where she raised her family last year. Over the ensuing weeks, she laboriously repeated the process of building a nest by starting once again on the right-hand side, working her way behind the meat platters before finally constructing a new nest in exactly the same place.

Friends and family came to visit, intrigued and fascinated by the dedication of this small bird. When Mrs R arrived carrying moss rather than leaves, I knew the nest was nearing completion. However, several days later having made a nice cosy hollow to receive the eggs, she abandoned it and has never come back.

My conclusion is that, unlike Mr R from last year, her new husband was unable to gain enough confidence to take on board his responsibilities, which meant coming into a busy house to look after his young. It was an impossible situation, and I can only hope that a new nest and family will have been established somewhere nearby where both parents feel safe and secure. Will Mrs R return next year to try again? We shall have to wait and see.